miffy and the impressionists

Front cover:
Georges Seurat, *Bathers at Asnières*, 1884.
Oil on canvas. 201 × 300 cm (24½ x 118⅛ in.).
The National Gallery, London/Scala, Florence

First published in the United Kingdom in 2026 by
Thames & Hudson Ltd, 6–24 Britannia Street, London WC1X 9JD

Publication licensed by Mercis Publishing bv, Amsterdam

Miffy and the Impressionists © 2026 Thames & Hudson Ltd, London

Text © 2026 Mercis Publishing bv
Illustrations by Dick Bruna © Mercis bv, 1953–2026
Photographs of Dick Bruna by Ferry André de la Porte © Mercis bv

All Rights Reserved. No part of this publication may be
reproduced or transmitted in any form or by any means,
electronic or mechanical, including photocopy, recording
or any other information storage and retrieval system,
without prior permission in writing from the publisher.

EU Authorized Representative: Interart S.A.R.L.
19 rue Charles Auray, 93500 Pantin, Paris, France
productsafety@thameshudson.co.uk
interart.fr

A CIP catalogue record for this book is available from the British Library

ISBN 978-0-500-65402-6
01

Printed and bound in China by Leo Paper Products Ltd.

Be the first to know about our new releases,
exclusive content and author events by visiting
thamesandhudson.com
thamesandhudsonusa.com
thamesandhudson.com.au

miffy and the impressionists

dick bruna

Join Miffy on an art adventure to discover paintings created by a group of artists known as the Impressionists. The Impressionists looked closely at the world around them, and created impressions of everyday moments, rather than depicting realistic scenes. They wanted to show how it feels to watch the sun rise over a landscape, or to see children playing on a beach.

Dick Bruna was also inspired by the world around him. The world he created for Miffy isn't realistic either – in his drawings he removed as many details as possible until he was left with only the lines that were essential. Throughout the world, children recognise his yellow circle as a sun, and a few lines as hills.

Look closely at the pairings in this book. At first glance the artworks might look nothing like Dick Bruna's work, but if you take your time, you'll start to see similarities. Discover new ways to look at art and get inspired by what you see!

Claude Monet was fascinated by steam engines.
He would sit at the train station and paint the giant,
puffing clouds of steam before they disappeared.

Miffy loves playing with her toy train.
Do you like trains, too?

Edgar Degas spent most of his life drawing and painting ballerinas practising their poses – bending, stretching, twirling and standing on their tiptoes.

Can you dance and point your toes like a ballerina?

Mary Cassatt wanted to remember her childhood
when she played in the sand with her sister,
so she made a painting of her memory.

Miffy also likes to play in the sand.
What do you like to do at the beach?

**Paul Signac was an artist and a sailor.
He loved the sea and owned 32 boats over his lifetime!
He used short brushstrokes of brightly coloured paint
to capture the sunlight reflecting on water.**

How many boats do you see in the painting?

**Alfred Sisley lived in the countryside
and loved working outdoors.**

**Look, the geese are following the gooseherd
just like the ducks are following Miffy!**

On a hot summer's day Georges Seurat sat down on the riverbank and sketched people going for a swim.

Is Miffy ready to jump in?

Auguste Renoir painted a girl in her best clothes, posing with her favourite toy.

What toy would you choose to pose with?

Berthe Morisot had to paint quickly with big brushstrokes to catch this girl cuddling her dog before it jumped off her lap.

Are both dogs asleep?

Camille Pissarro lived on a farm with an orchard.
He liked to watch and paint the apple pickers at work.
The apples look delicious!

What is your favourite fruit?

Gustave Caillebotte painted the bustling city.
On grey and rainy days the streets
looked wet and shiny.

Boris is lucky he brought his umbrella.
How can you tell it's raining?

Édouard Manet thought it was important to paint pictures of ordinary things in everyday life. This little girl wants to help her mother wash the clothes with soap.

Miffy likes to wash herself with soapy bubbles!

Claude Monet's eldest son liked to ride his horse tricycle around the garden. One day Monet asked his son to stop pedalling so he could paint a picture of him.

Miffy likes to ride her bike.
Can you count the wheels on her bicycle?
And on the horse tricycle?

meet the impressionists

The Impressionists were a group of artists who used art to capture the fleeting moments in everyday life. They developed new techniques – including painting outdoors with quick brushstrokes – to capture the way people moved, and changes in the light and weather.

Dimensions of works are given in centimetres and inches, height before width.

Claude Monet
1840–1926, France

The Gare Saint-Lazare: Arrival of a Train, 1877. Oil on canvas. 83 x 101.3 cm (32¹¹⁄₁₆ x 39⅞ in.). Harvard Art Museums/Bequest from the Collection of Maurice Wertheim, Class of 1906/Bridgeman Images

Edgar Degas
1834–1917, France

Two Dancers on a Stage, 1874. Oil on canvas. 61.5 x 46 cm (24¼ x 18⅛ in.). The Courtauld Institute of Art

Mary Cassatt
1844–1926, USA

Children Playing on the Beach, 1884. Oil on canvas. 97.4 × 74.2 cm (38⅜ × 29³⁄₁₆ in.). Ailsa Mellon Bruce Collection/National Gallery of Art, Washington, DC (1970.17.19)

Paul Signac
1863–1935, France

The Golden Horn. The Bridge, 1907. Oil on canvas. Dimensions unknown. Private Collection. Heritage Image Partnership Ltd/Alamy Stock Photo

Alfred Sisley
1839–1899, UK/France

The Geese in Saint-Mammès, c. 1885. Oil on canvas. 32.8 x 40.8 cm (12⅞ x 16⅛ in.). Private Collection. incamerastock/Alamy Stock Photo

Georges Seurat
1859–1891, France

Bathers at Asnières, 1884. Oil on canvas. 201 × 300 cm (24¼ x 118⅛ in.). The National Gallery, London/Scala, Florence

Auguste Renoir
1841–1919, France

Girl with a Hoop, 1885. Oil on canvas. 125.7 x 76.6 cm (49½ x 30³⁄₁₆ in.). Chester Dale Collection, National Gallery of Art, Washington DC (1963.10.58)

Berthe Morisot
1841–1895, France

Young Girl with a Dog, c. 1887. Oil on canvas. 78.8 x 60.1 cm (31 x 23⅝ in.). Private Collection. Alamy Stock Photo

Camille Pissarro
1830–1903, Denmark/France

Apple Picking, 1886. Oil on canvas. 125.8 x 127.4 cm (49½ x 50⅛ in.). Ohara Museum of Art, Kurashiki, Japan

Gustave Caillebotte
1848–1894, France

Paris Street; Rainy Day, 1877. Oil on canvas. 212.2 × 276.2 cm (83½ × 108¾ in.). Charles H. and Mary F. S. Worcester Collection/Art Institute of Chicago (1964.336) akg-images

Édouard Manet
1832–1883, France

Laundry (Le Linge), 1875. Oil on canvas. 145.4 x 114.9 cm (57¼ x 45¼ in.). The Barnes Foundation (BF957)

Claude Monet
1840–1926, France

Jean Monet (1867–1914) on His Horse Tricycle, 1872. Oil on canvas. 60.6 x 74.3 cm (23⅞ x 29¼ in.). Gift of Sara Lee Corporation, 2000/The Metropolitan Museum of Art, New York

meet dick bruna

Dick Bruna's illustration style is immediately recognisable because of its simplicity and universal appeal. The simplicity leaves plenty of room for children to use their own imagination.

Dick Bruna's work is characterised by thick black outlines drawn with a paintbrush (which show the 'heartbeat' of the artist) and vibrant colours. His confident lines convey a sense of warmth, combined with a subtle tenderness.